GUIDE TO PORTFOLIOS

Creating and Using Portfolios for Academic, Career, and Personal Success

Mary Robins
Menlo College

Boston   Columbus   Indianapolis   New York   San Francisco   Upper Saddle River
Amsterdam   Cape Town   Dubai   London   Madrid   Milan   Munich   Paris   Montreal   Toronto
Delhi   Mexico City   Sao Paulo   Sydney   Hong Kong   Seoul   Singapore   Taipei   Tokyo

Vice President and Editor in Chief: Jeffery Johnston

Acquisitions Editor: Sande Johnson

Editorial Assistant: Lynda Cramer

Vice President, Director of Marketing and Sales: Emily Williams Knight

Vice President, Director of Marketing: Quinn Perkson

Marketing Manager: Amy Judd

Marketing Coordinator: Brian Mounts

Senior Managing Editor: Pamela D. Bennett

Project Manager: Kerry J. Rubadue

Senior Operations Supervisor: Matthew Ottenweller

Art Director: Candace Rowley

Cover Designer: Candace Rowley

Cover Art: iStockphoto, Shutterstock

Full-Service Project Management: Thistle Hill Publishing Services, LLC

Composition: Integra

Printer/Binder: Bind-Rite Graphics/Robbinsville

Cover Printer: Lehigh Phoenix Color/Hagerstown

Text Font: Berkeley

Photo Credits: p. 1, Dean Mitchell/Shutterstock; p. 3, Keith Brofsky/Getty Images, Inc.–Photodisc; p. 13, Shutterstock; p. 19, Shutterstock.

Credits and acknowledgments borrowed from other sources and reproduced, with permission, in this textbook appear on appropriate page within text.

Every effort has been made to provide accurate and current Internet information in this book. However, the Internet and information posted on it are constantly changing, so it is inevitable that some of the Internet addresses listed in this textbook will change.

Library of Congress Cataloging-in-Publication Data

Robins, Mary.
  Guide to portfolios : creating and using portfolios for academic, career, and personal success / Mary Robins.
      p. cm.
  Includes bibliographical references.
  ISBN-13: 978-0-13-714533-1 (pbk.)
  ISBN-10: 0-13-714533-0 (pbk.)
  1. Portfolios in education.   2. Career development.   3. Vocational guidance.
I. Title.
LB1029.P67R63 2010
371.39—dc22

                                                        2009016074

10 9 8 7 6 5 4 3 2 1

www.pearsonhighered.com

ISBN 13: 978-0-13-714533-1
ISBN 10:   0-13-714533-0

LEARNING OBJECTIVES FOR *GUIDE TO PORTFOLIOS*

The objectives for *Guide to Portfolios* are listed below. They have been developed to guide you, the reader, to the core issues covered in this book.

Objectives:

1. To explain the functions of four categories of portfolios: Master Portfolio, Assessment Portfolios, Career Portfolios, and Personal Portfolios.
2. To help you determine which portfolio to use in different situations.
3. To describe how to create and present a portfolio.

ABOUT THE AUTHOR

Mary Robins is the director of Career Services at Menlo College, a small business college in Atherton, California. As director, Mary works with a variety of students of all ages and work/life experiences. Mary's career has included working as a human resource manager and marketing manager in the consumer publishing industry. She has a B.S. in Human Services with an emphasis in counseling from Notre Dame de Namur University and a M.A. in Career Development from John F. Kennedy University's School of Management. Mary is a past president of the California Career Development Association and a frequent presenter at career conferences.

ACKNOWLEDGMENTS

Many people have supported me in writing this book. I am extremely grateful to my husband, John, who provided me with a loving home throughout the process. I'd also like to thank my two wonderful daughters, Amy and Lisa, who listened to me and provided encouragement and feedback.

At work I have many people to thank. First of all is Michelle Beese, with whom I had the pleasure of coteaching a course to our NDNU students on Developing a Career Portfolio. We had two other professors joining us in this project, Dr. Christine Bennett and Dr. Sandra Bernhard, who as a result of this course helped share our vision of portfolios with other faculty. And, thanks to Sue Aiken, who patiently guided me through my initial research and development of the project when I was attending JFKU's Career Development program.

A special thanks to the "Portfolio Mavens"—Michelle Beese, Carmen Croonquist, Gina Larson, Kate Dutro, and Kassia Dellabough. This wonderful group of women provides a community in which we all explore the concept of portfolios.

I would also like to thank the following reviewers: Phyllis Bickers, Auburn University; Karen Ervin, DeVry University; Victoria Gatsiopoulos, Kaplan Career Institute, ICM Campus; and Beth Humes, Pennsylvania Culinary Institute.

CONTENTS

INTRODUCTION

I created my first portfolio back in the 1990s when I was working as a marketing manager for a major publishing company. My department's goal was to support our salespeople in their efforts to sell advertising space in our magazine. We did this by producing very creative business-to-business direct-mail programs to the target group selected by our advertiser. Over the course of six years, I had the opportunity to design and produce creative mailers and packages for some of the largest and best-known organizations in the United States and Canada, including General Foods, Ralston Purina, General Mills, Ford Motor Company, Travel Alberta, and Jenn-Air. I began to collect samples and pictures of the direct-mail campaigns I worked on, keeping some in a box and putting others in a portfolio similar to those that freelance designers had shown me.

As I moved from one division of the company to another, I continued to add to my portfolio. In my next job, my responsibilities included managing trade shows, publicity, and trade and consumer promotions. Again, I kept press releases, sales sheets, and photographs from projects I had worked on and added them to my portfolio.

When it came time to look for a new job, I created a new portfolio with my resume and the best examples of my work so that I could show potential employers the depth of my marketing experience. I included examples of four-color catalogs I worked on, sales sheets showing display materials I had produced, advertising copy I had written, photographs of trade show booths I had designed, and press releases I had written for special events. I was prepared to take my portfolio on all my interviews. However, I actually used my portfolio at only one organization—they offered me the job! (I still use that portfolio today to help college students understand the variety of marketing tasks they will execute when working in a marketing department.)

Over the next few years, I continued to maintain my portfolio, collecting samples and adding a few of them to a binder. However, my next big portfolio came in a totally different setting—school. In order to further my career and open up opportunities, I returned to school to get my bachelor's degree. In my capstone class, one of the assignments was to create a portfolio that reflected what I had learned over the course of the program.

This portfolio took on a life of its own. Once I got started pulling together papers and tests from my classes, I found it hard to stop. Three inches thick, my "academic" portfolio includes my acceptance letter, transcripts, awards, class lists, syllabi, and papers. Once completed, I felt an amazing sense of accomplishment. It was great to see the portfolios that each of my classmates created. Although we had been given the same assignment and instructions, each one of us created a portfolio that was unique and very personal. As we each reflected on the experience of creating our portfolios, some students mentioned that they had shown their portfolios to colleagues at work to help them understand the academic program, others had shown their portfolios to potential employers, and others had shown it to family and friends. Everyone in the class felt that the energy it took to assemble the portfolio was well worth the time and the effort.

Once I got started on portfolios, I was hooked. I began to see how they could be created and used with a variety of audiences. This book was created to help individuals like you navigate the process of creating portfolios. While doing research on portfolios, I found that at times different names are used for the same portfolios, and different types of portfolios sometimes were called the same thing. It became quite confusing. As a result, I have tried to differentiate portfolios based on the intended audience and the purpose. The major distinctions made are between the master portfolio, which keeps everything together, the assessment portfolios, which are used in academic settings in order to assess learning, career portfolios, which are used in employment situations, and personal portfolios, which are used strictly for your own self-discovery and enrichment.

A portfolio can have an enormous personal and professional impact on your life. A portfolio can provide you with a measurement of your abilities without taking a test. A portfolio can provide documentation of your skills to a group of people who will award you a certification based on your demonstrated skills and knowledge. A portfolio can help a graduate school admissions advisor better understand who you are as a student and a person. A portfolio can set you apart from the competition when you are applying for a job. And, a portfolio can show your supervisor how well you have met your goals and objectives for a performance review period.

Regardless of the reason why you create your first portfolio, once you've created it, you'll most likely begin dreaming up situations in which you could use other types of portfolios. That's what happened to me.

ABOUT THIS BOOK

Section I of this book will give you a broad overview of portfolios, their history, and definition. You'll be asked to think about how and why you might benefit from creating a portfolio.

Section II explores the audiences who might look at your portfolio and how that will influence what you collect and how you put your portfolio together.

Section III provides you with simple and easy steps for creating your portfolio. The steps are designed to be used for any category or type of portfolio.

Section IV provides you with worksheets and exercises to help you create each type of portfolio, as well as strategies for presenting your portfolio to others. Many of these pages are reproducible and can be copied as often as needed.

What Is a Portfolio?

Portfolios have come to mean different things to different people. There is often confusion when talking to people about portfolios because of these different interpretations. In this section of the book, you will find definitions of portfolios based on the intended audience. Once the audience has been identified, the purpose and type of portfolio become clearer.

WHAT DO YOU THINK OF WHEN YOU HEAR THE WORD "PORTFOLIO"?

If you are a student you may already be familiar with portfolios from one of your classes, or perhaps this is an entirely new concept for you. If you have been involved in remodeling a home, an architect or designer may have showed you a portfolio of past work. If you have hired a graphic designer to design some artwork, she may have shown you her portfolio of samples from past jobs. If you have children, you may be thinking of the portfolio your child created for a school project.

All of these are examples of "portfolios." But, what is a portfolio?

If you look up *portfolio* in Webster's dictionary you will find that a portfolio is defined as "a flat portable case for carrying loose papers, drawings, etc. or the contents or such a case, especially a collection of drawings, photographs, etc. representative of a person's work." This definition clearly points back to the origin of a portfolio as a tool used by artists to secure work.

However, in the last decade, other groups have expanded the concept. Now, a portfolio has come to mean any collection of artifacts—samples of work, photographs, papers, testimonials— that an individual purposefully compiles to create a visual documentation of her or his accomplishments.

WHY CREATE A PORTFOLIO?

There are many reasons you may want or need to create a portfolio. A portfolio is a wonderful tool to use when you want to document your academic learning, the skills and competencies you have learned in school or on the job, your achievements, and even your own personal growth over time. Once assembled, you can share your portfolio with others or simply keep it as a personal document.

Below I've listed some reasons for creating a portfolio. Check all that you see may apply to you at some point in your life. Add any others reasons you can think of at the bottom of the list.

❑ A school assignment
❑ Document a successful event or project
❑ Show a potential employer that you have the appropriate skills and competencies to do a job
❑ Convince a potential customer of your range of talents and creative ideas
❑ Show your children or grandchildren highlights from your personal and professional life
❑ Distinguish yourself from the competition
❑ Prove your skill and competency for certification
❑ Impress your graduate school admissions advisor
❑ Take stock of your own accomplishments
❑ Keep track of your finished work and recommendation letters
❑ _____
❑ _____
❑ _____

These are just some ideas on why you might want to create a portfolio. There are many others. Brainstorm with friends and family to discover additional reasons to create and use a portfolio.

Different Portfolios for Different Audiences

P ortfolios are similar to speeches. In order to maximize effectiveness you must first decide who is your audience. For example, if I were going to give a speech on how to grow roses to a youth group and a garden club, the content and tone of the speech would be adapted and be appropriate for each audience.

You develop a speech or a portfolio by determining what your audience is looking for and what will capture their imagination and keep their attention focused on you. The most common audiences for a portfolio are: teachers, professors, hiring managers, supervisors, or yourself. Based on these audiences, I've divided the portfolio into four categories: Master Portfolio, Assessment Portfolios, Career Portfolios, and Personal Portfolios.

Over time you may have multiple portfolios depending upon your own personal needs. You may find that you use many of the same artifacts in different portfolios, but you may place them in a different section or in a different order. You may want to combine portfolio types to suit your own unique situation. Knowing how to create each of the different portfolios will help you in the future.

> **TIP:** Begin by saving everything. Once you have many examples you can begin to thin out your materials. As time goes on you can replace an item with a better example.

We will discuss the four portfolio categories: Master Portfolio, Assessment Portfolio, Career Portfolio, and Personal Portfolio.

1. MASTER PORTFOLIO

I've been keeping a Master Portfolio for each of the past three years. At the beginning of each academic year, I set up a new binder, put in tabs for each month, and stock it with plastic sleeves. I keep it on the shelf behind my desk and add two to five artifacts each month. In years past, I have pulled out the best samples of my work and created a performance portfolio, sharing it with my manager during my annual performance review. I've also referred back to my Master Portfolio to find examples of marketing materials and letters I can use to help me come up with new ideas for this year's projects. I love my job, but I also know that if I decided to move to another job, I could pull items from my Master Portfolio and create a dynamic Resume-based Portfolio. As I review my portfolio at the end of the year, I'm proud of what I've accomplished.

When I first began writing about portfolios, I didn't see the need for a Master Portfolio. I felt that if you are going to create a portfolio, you should already know why you're doing it. After talking with many people and having more experience with portfolios, I've come to understand the benefits of having a process to collect artifacts on an ongoing basis.

The Audience   You are the audience for your Master Portfolio. However, when it's time to pull artifacts and put them in another portfolio, a second pair of eyes might help you see things that you don't see.

The Purpose and Objectives   The Master Portfolio allows you keep and organize artifacts even if you don't have an immediate need to create a specific portfolio. One of the hardest things about putting a portfolio together is gathering the artifacts. If you've already thrown away wonderful examples of your work, you may not have the opportunity to replace them. The one comment I heard from students who took my Portfolio class was, "I wish I'd started saving things when I was a freshman."

The Benefits   Besides creating an organizational tool to collect artifacts, a Master Portfolio gives you a great opportunity to check in with your academic or career path. Because you'll generally save the items that you are most proud of, by looking at them as a whole you will begin to see patterns. These patterns may help point you in the direction of your next step in your academic or professional career.

What You Need to Know   The best way to avoid not having the artifacts you really want is to just begin saving. Save everything. If later on you find an artifact that is a better example of your skills, you can toss the earlier one. When you're ready to create the specific portfolio, then you can pull the appropriate artifacts from your Master Portfolio to put in your new portfolio.

> **TIP:** Set up your Master Portfolio by month and plan to save at least two or three items each month.

As you collect the artifacts, take a moment and record information about the piece while it is still fresh in your mind. One way to do this is to write an accomplishment statement, or STAR. STAR stands for situation (S), task (T), action you took (A), and results (R). To begin your STAR, start with a story. You can either record the story yourself or ask a friend to write it down for you while you tell it. If someone else records the story, encourage her to ask questions for clarification. Once the story has been written down, look to see what talents or skills you used. Note the specific action you took and the results. Whenever possible, use specific statistics such as the number of people you served, the dollar amount of the budget you managed, or the percentage increase in sales you made. If you don't capture this information when it happens, it may be difficult or impossible to get later. Finally, attach this statement to the artifact and add it to your portfolio.

An important part of keeping a Master Portfolio is to set a time at least once a year to review what you've added to the portfolio. This is a great time to be sure that you've also captured information about each artifact and to notice whether you're missing anything.

TIP: At the end of the year, add your personal and work calendars to your collection. You can use them to help trigger memories of things you worked on during the year.

---

2. ASSESSMENT PORTFOLIOS—ACADEMIC AND TECHNICAL

Kristy always wanted to teach. After graduating from college, her next step was to apply to graduate school. She collected a variety of materials that she had used with students in volunteer positions in college and created a portfolio that she could share with the graduate school admissions team. Her portfolio included her personal statement, photographs of the children she worked with, and exercises that she had used with the children. The manner in which she assembled the portfolio—using bright colors and child-friendly graphics—demonstrated her creativity. When she showed her graduate school admissions counselor her portfolio, the response was extremely positive. The counselor not only had a sense of Kristy's commitment to teaching, but also knew that she'd have no difficulty compiling a new portfolio, which was a requirement of the teaching credential program.

Academic Portfolios

The portfolio movement got a boost in the mid-1990s as more and more teachers began to ask their students to create an academic or assessment portfolio as part of their own classroom activities. You can now find teachers at all levels—from elementary to high school to college—incorporating portfolios into their teaching and assessment process.

Some teachers ask their students to keep a working portfolio, an intentional collection of school work in progress or finished that is guided by learning objectives. The work stays in the working portfolio until it is ready to be moved to a display or assessment portfolio. Other teachers ask their students to create a display or assessment portfolio—a collection of only the best work for the year, showing that a student has mastered the curriculum and is eligible for promotion to the next class or grade level. Portfolios may cover one class, one semester or quarter, one year, or even a two- to four-year period.

The Audience   The audience for an academic portfolio is your teacher or school, yourself, and your family. The teacher or school will suggest or even require what is to be included in the portfolio. For example, you may be required to include papers from all your classes, as well as flyers, programs, reflection papers, and photographs from extracurricular activities.

The Purpose and Objective   The actual purpose of the portfolio may vary. Check with your teacher or school to understand the objectives of your specific portfolio. Usually, the purpose will be to assess learning over a specified period of time. Other objectives of the portfolio may be to motivate and encourage goal setting, inform parents and family of your skills and knowledge, engage you in your own learning, help you learn the skills of reflection and self-evaluation, or document your learning in areas that do not lend themselves to traditional assessment.

The Benefits   There are many benefits to creating an assessment portfolio. Creating a portfolio will give you an opportunity to reflect on your academic and personal growth, provide you with an awareness and satisfaction in your accomplishments, and help you build connections between courses, cocurricular activities, and career opportunities. Most importantly it also allows you to take responsibility for being an active, thoughtful participant in the analysis and assessment of your own learning.

What You Need to Know   Let's say that your professor has asked you to keep a portfolio as part of your class assignments. Perhaps the portfolio will represent a major part of your grade. What would you include in it?

The first item you should include would be the class syllabus. The teacher may also provide you with specific assignments that should be included in the portfolio. But most likely he would also encourage you to add your own items that show what make you unique.

In my Career Management class, the majority of the students' grades are based on their Career Portfolio. Throughout the semester, my students complete a series of assessments and exercises and write papers on a variety of career exploration experiences, such as conducting an information interview or attending a career fair. I also provide handouts about the career management process that will be helpful to them later on. I provide them with a list of materials that must be included in the portfolio, but I also encourage them to include other materials that are relevant. One of the things I look for when grading the portfolio is whether it is presented professionally and well organized.

Look for a list of competencies or learning that is included on handouts or the syllabus and discussed by the teacher. Some colleges, such as Alverno College in Wisconsin, have created a matrix of skills for each academic year. The matrix is found on the school's Web site and is accessible to all students. You can find more information about Alverno's diagnostic digital portfolio at *www.alverno.edu*. The site describes the portfolio:

> This first-of-its-kind, web-based system [that] enables each Alverno student—anyplace, anytime—to follow her learning progress throughout her years of study. It helps the student process the feedback she receives from faculty, external assessors and peers. It also enables her to look for patterns in her academic work so she can take more control of her own development and become a more autonomous learner. The Diagnostic Digital Portfolio (DDP) is built on Alverno's student assessment-as-learning process, making it more transparent to the student and others who seek to understand this important educational program. It also provides actual, accessible performance data with which graduates can create an electronic resume for potential employers or for graduate schools.

Alverno College's online portfolio has become a model for other colleges and universities.

I have found that some faculty members ask students to create a Career Portfolio but at the same time ask students to include materials that would not be appropriate in a portfolio taken on a job interview. For example, the professor may ask you to include photos or reflections from cocurricular activities. While some examples may be appropriate, many may not be. This is when the concept of the audience really comes into play. Regardless of the title of the portfolio, you should include the materials that your professor requires.

Technical Portfolios

Professional associations and governmental licensing boards are also embracing portfolios. For these governing bodies, a portfolio solves a practical issue. How do you assess the knowledge and skills of members in a large geographic area who are applying for certification, credentials, or a license? The portfolio allows the individual to come to the governing body. A portfolio also provides candidates with the opportunity to show creative examples of their work that go beyond the true/false and multiple-choice questions answered on an exam.

The Audience   The audience for a Technical Portfolio is the governing body who oversees the portfolio assessment portion of the certification, credential, or licensing process. Therefore, it is this group who determines what must be included in the portfolio. The governing body may ask you to include and demonstrate through artifacts or evidence the basic skills and competencies established for all practicing members of the organization.

The Purpose and Objectives   Your objective for maintaining a Technical Portfolio is to provide information and evidence of your skills and competencies. This may take place as you launch your career or as you maintain your professional standing.

Most professional associations, certification bodies, and governmental licensing boards require individuals to continue their education in order to maintain their professional standing. Individuals can earn continuing education units (CEUs) by participating in workshops, taking classes, or attending conferences. Just as the International Association of Continuing Education and Training (IACET) requires all of its CEU providers to maintain records of CEU completion for seven years, an association also often requires members to maintain and produce their record of completed coursework over a specific period of time. A portfolio is a great way for individuals to organize their CEUs.

The Benefits   Whether you create a portfolio may not be an option. Your ability to prove your competencies may be necessary for you to move on to the next level of your career or keep you in current standing with your professional organization.

What You Need to Know   Colleges and universities with teacher education programs often require their student teachers to keep Technical Portfolios based on competencies established by a state board of education. For example, Notre Dame de Namur University's School of Education has developed guidelines to help its student teachers with the process of developing a standards-based portfolio based on the California Standards for the Teaching Profession (CSTP). The six standards are:

- Engaging and supporting all students in learning
- Creating and maintaining effective environments for student learning
- Understanding and organizing subject matter for student learning
- Planning instruction and designing learning experiences for all students
- Assessing student learning
- Developing as a professional educator

To make the portfolio unique to its program, Notre Dame de Namur University also requires its student teachers to add elements to their portfolios that support the mission and core values of the university, such as:

- A commitment to develop one's full potential (the whole person)
- A commitment to build an interactive, interdisciplinary community of learners (the collaborative community)
- A commitment to enhance justice and peace at the personal, communal, and global levels (the just society)
- The lifelong development of core competencies: human development skills, communication skills, and thinking skills

When researching this book, I found that a wide variety of professional associations and teacher education programs require a portfolio as part of the graduation requirement or to maintain professional standing.

If your professional or trade association requires you to complete continuing education units, be sure you get the appropriate paperwork signed immediately after the educational event and then add it to your portfolio. While the organization putting on the event is required to keep records of your attendance, it may take time and money to retrieve the information later. It's your responsibility to produce evidence of your CEUs to your association in a timely manner.

In some cases, you may decide to create a portfolio on your own to showcase your credentials, skills, and accomplishments based on the competencies dictated by a professional organization. For example, the National Career Development Association describes competencies in eleven areas that an individual must demonstrate in order to work as a professional engaged in career counseling. Among the eleven areas are career development theory, individual and group counseling skills, individual/group assessment, information and resources, diverse populations, technology, and ethical/legal issues. Keeping this type of portfolio is a great way for a career counselor to make sure he is keeping current with his skills.

These are some examples of how portfolios are used in academic venues and in professional organizations. As portfolios become more and more widely used, more opportunities will most likely be invented.

3. CAREER PORTFOLIOS—RESUME-BASED, PROJECT, AND PERFORMANCE

Tom, a graduating senior in Mass Communications, was looking for his first full-time job after college. While he had lots of great experiences as a student, the part-time jobs he held while attending school didn't match the objective on his resume. At the urging of his college career counselor, Tom put together a portfolio of the projects he had completed in his classes and as a student leader. The finished portfolio gave him the confidence and the proof he needed to approach potential employers. Tom is now happily a Web master and is using the skills he learned in college.

Resume-based Portfolios

Resume-based Portfolios differ from assessment portfolios in one significant way—the audience. It is important to acknowledge this difference because artifacts and documents that may have been appropriate for a teacher or school may pose a problem for a potential or current employer.

The Audience   The audience for a Resume-based Portfolio is an individual within an organization, such as a hiring manager, department manager, or supervisor. The resume-based portfolio helps bring a resume to life and should enhance and support the accomplishments and key skills in the resume. It is important to note that because hiring managers are going out of their way to avoid any sense of discrimination in hiring practices, you do not want to include any photo or document in your portfolio that shows your race, age, religious or political affiliation, or family. As a rule of thumb, if something isn't appropriate on your resume, it may not be appropriate in your portfolio. However, the choice is always yours.

The Purpose and Objectives   The purpose and the goal of the Resume-based Portfolio is to help you demonstrate and verify your work experiences to potential employers and to help you stand out from the competition. A Resume-based Portfolio can be effective to help you find a new job either within your current company or outside your organization.

> **TIP:** College students may not always have examples from their work experience. If not, include examples from activities that you've been involved in on campus, such as a club event, class presentation, or residence hall project. If you've already graduated from college, perhaps you've been involved with an event or project in a volunteer capacity. It still counts, so be sure to include artifacts from these events in your portfolio.

The Benefits   The benefits for creating a Resume-based Portfolio are twofold. The most important benefit is in the process itself. In combination with creating your resume, your portfolio provides you with an opportunity to reflect and decide on what you truly want to do in the future. It also provides you with an opportunity to consider a time when you have used particular skills or competencies on the job. This reflection will come in handy if the hiring manager uses behavioral interviewing techniques—the concept that past performance predicts future performance. Even if you don't have the opportunity to share your portfolio in the interview, you will approach the interview with more confidence in your proven abilities and skills.

The second benefit is that you will stand out from the competition. Portfolios are an overlooked concept in the job search process and only a small number of applicants are taking advantage of this powerful tool. By bringing your portfolio on the interview and referencing it on your resume, you show the hiring manager that you have carefully thought out your career goals and abilities. It is important to remember though, that your portfolio can't take your place on the interview—it's still up to you to make a great impression.

What You Need to Know   Yana Parker, author of *The Damn Good Resume Guide,* wrote: "your resume is about the future, not about the past." Just as you write your resume based on what you want to do in the future, your Resume-based Portfolio will also reflect what you want and can bring to an organization.

When you create a Resume-based Portfolio, you want to include artifacts that support specific skills and competencies that you have mastered and want to use again. For example, when I was a human resource manager, I was responsible for handling payroll. While I was good at payroll, it's not a job I'd like to do in the future, so you won't find anything about it either on my resume or in my portfolio.

> **TIP:** Your Resume-based Portfolio should be no thicker than a half-inch to 1 inch. You don't want to overwhelm a hiring manager by bringing in a thick binder. Bringing a thick portfolio to a job interview might actually raise a red flag because you may not appear focused or able to succinctly summarize your skills.

To help you determine your skills, competencies, and strengths, you may want to meet with a career counselor who has tools and exercises such as SkillScan by Beckhusen and Gazzano or the Motivated Skill Sort by Dick Knowdell and other exercises to help you identify your key skills. You can also find information about skills in career books, such as *What Color Is Your Parachute,* by Richard Bolles, and *The Complete Job-Search Handbook,* by Howard Figler, Ph.D.

Once you know what skills you have and what skills you want to develop further, you will also want to see which skills employers are looking for from candidates. The best place to find these skills is in job ads, job postings, and job descriptions. As you read through the job listing, take note of the specific skills and behaviors the employer has included in the ad, and then if these are skills you have and would like to use in the future, be sure they appear in your resume and in your portfolio.

> **TIP:** Write down all the skills and behaviors included in an ad, then note which you already have, which you need to learn, and which you don't want to use in the future.

Project Portfolios

A Project Portfolio helps you or a group keep track of key elements of a project such as the budget, resources, marketing materials, evaluations, and suggestions for improvement. It's the only portfolio that a group might contribute to rather than just one individual.

The Audience   The audience for this type of portfolio is a person or group currently working on a project or a group that will be formed in the future to duplicate the project or use the past project as a resource.

The Purpose and Objective   The purpose of this type of portfolio is to help another group or team replicate the project. Or, the portfolio may be created strictly as a historical record.

The Benefits   The benefits of a project portfolio are well known to those who have tried to replicate a project with no documentation from the previous effort. Rather than starting from scratch, a new team can review the prior budget, resources, and marketing plans. Problems that may have surfaced in the first project may be more easily avoided in the second. Changes to the program can be made based on feedback from those involved helping to increase the success. Time can also be saved because forms and marketing materials can be updated and used again.

What You Need to Know   Organization is the key. Develop your portfolio so anyone can pick it up and easily understand what has happened in the past.

Consider setting up your Project Portfolio by using the steps within the project—project initiation, planning or design stage, production stage, and evaluation. If it's a large project with many team members, poll the group to get their input and suggestions.

Performance Portfolios

For many in the workforce, getting an annual salary increase isn't guaranteed even if you're doing a great job. How do you show value to budget decision makers up the line who aren't in direct contact with you day to day? Michelle decided to create a Performance Portfolio. Guided by her performance objectives, Michelle collected artifacts that proved she had completed her objectives. She included statistics, project handouts, evaluations, and testimonials. When Michelle's boss went in for the budget meeting with his boss, he was not only able to speak about Michelle's value, but by using her portfolio he was also able to show it. Pictures are worth a thousand words, and sometimes they are also worth a raise!

One of the hottest topics in business is performance management. Organizations struggle with establishing an approach that benefits both the company and the employee. A Performance Portfolio is one way an organization shifts some of the responsibility of documenting performance from the supervisor to the employee.

The Audience   The audience for the Performance Portfolio is the employee and his or her supervisor. The portfolio may be shared with other individuals within the organization.

The Purpose and Objectives   The purpose of the Performance Portfolio is to provide you with a tool that allows you to document your performance. It can be created and used even if your organization handles performance reviews in a different way or not at all.

> **TIP:** Save at least five extra copies of printed materials to make sure you have extras should you ever need them.

The Benefits   There are many benefits to a Performance Portfolio. Although you may only intend to use this portfolio with your immediate supervisor, don't be surprised if she asks to show it to her boss. It is a great way to show off the accomplishments not only of one worker, but also of an entire department.

Your Performance Portfolio is also a good way to back up your case for a merit increase. Rather than talking with your supervisor in general terms about your accomplishments and contributions to the organization, your portfolio provides documented evidence of your impact.

Other benefits of the Performance Portfolio are more personal. By looking through your portfolio you can quickly identify your strengths, as well as any skill areas that need improvement. Your portfolio also provides you with a place to store certificates or CEUs you may receive for attending specialized training or awards you have won. Should you decide to change jobs, you have already collected samples of your best work that can be moved to a Resume-based Portfolio. And finally, there is often personal gratification in looking back over your work to see how much you have grown personally and professionally.

What You Need to Know   An approach to performance management that is being adopted by organizations is one in which the employee and supervisor sit down at the beginning of the performance period and together determine goals and objectives for a specific period of time.

The discussion might include key roles and responsibilities, goals, barriers, and measurable outcomes. Throughout the performance period, adjustments are made to the performance plan based on changing business conditions. When the time for the actual review comes, the employee takes the lead and presents information and documentation about his or her performance to the supervisor. A Performance Portfolio that provides specific artifacts or documents strengthens this process.

One area of caution: Some individuals work in a field or organization where the work product is confidential, proprietary, or owned by the organization. You never want to include any materials in your portfolio that are confidential or proprietary. When creating your portfolio, you may need to be creative about what you include and perhaps even include a nondisclosure agreement or statement of originality. As an example, you might include the company's annual report and an accomplishment statement that tells how you contributed to the company's overall goals.

Career Portfolios are still a relatively new concept. Some employers aren't quite sure what to do with them, while others are embracing the idea and looking to hire individuals who have created portfolios. Time will tell as to whether or not portfolios will become a larger part of professional lives.

> **TIP:** Include a copy of your job description in your Performance Portfolio. Make a list of key skills and goals that you'd like to show your supervisor.

4. PERSONAL PORTFOLIOS—PERSONAL PORTFOLIOS, THE SCRAPBOOK

When Kassia decided to explore her next career move, she decided to create a portfolio. Rather than being structured and having a preconceived idea of what the portfolio would be, she decided to keep the portfolio organic. She wanted to first collect and assemble what was important to her and then see what story it told. She had no idea going into the portfolio what she would discover by completing it. Many of the artifacts in Kassia's portfolio are large, and others are compiled into collages. She has included artwork, papers from work, photos, poems she has written, ticket stubs, and other items. While each piece is important, it was the bigger picture that was most revealing. She then used what she learned from her portfolio to make decisions on her personal and professional life.

Erica was looking for a house in a tough rental market. To get a jump on her competition, she decided to pull together all the materials that a landlord would require when considering a new tenant. She included items such as references from previous landlords, personal references, financial information, personal philosophy, and contact information. Erica found her perfect house and, before the tour was over, produced her small portfolio. The owner was so impressed with her thoughtfulness, initiative, and professionalism that he rented the house to her.

Personal Portfolios

A Personal Portfolio or Scrapbook is created for the delight, satisfaction, and discovery of the individual. It may be a combination of the assessment or career portfolios, or perhaps it contains items that are strictly personal and deal with home and family. I know of one individual who created a portfolio just to show her grandchildren the career path she had taken. The Personal Portfolio may include artifacts such as personal pictures and mementos that may not be appropriate in an assessment or career portfolio.

The Audience   The audience for a Personal Portfolio is completely up to you. You can create it just for yourself or for your family. You may want to create a portfolio for a specific task, such as getting an apartment or handling a health issue.

The Purpose and Objective   The purpose of the Personal Portfolio is wide open—the portfolio can be created for whatever reasons you want and need. The benefits of creating this type of portfolio will depend on its purpose, and I believe it is safe to say that everyone who creates a portfolio comes away from the experience with a greater appreciation for who they are and what they have accomplished.

The Benefits   There are so many pressures in life—school, work, family, community. A Personal Portfolio allows you take the time to stop and evaluate what's important. It allows you to document all aspects of your life and keep them for posterity. And for many, a Personal Portfolio provides a creative outlet you may not have in your work life.

What You Need to Know   While you may have a specific reason to create a Personal Portfolio like documenting a trip or getting an apartment, don't overlook the power of creating a portfolio as a vehicle for self-exploration and discovery. By taking the time to sift through items that are important to you, you'll discover your passion and joy in life. If you keep yourself open to the possibilities, you may either confirm what you already know or find surprises that have a lasting impact. And, you may leave your portfolio as a legacy to be shared with parents, children, or even grandchildren.

Creating Your Portfolio

LET'S GET STARTED: DETERMINE THE AUDIENCE FOR YOUR PORTFOLIO

Now that you know the types of portfolios, it's time to begin thinking about creating a portfolio. Let's start with the audience that you'd like to show your portfolio to.

In the space below, write down the audience for your portfolio. Include everything you know about them. Remember, this is a bit like writing a speech. You may want to do research to confirm your knowledge or add more information. Some types of information you might want to include are:

- Names of individuals to whom you will present your portfolio.
- Titles or positions of these individuals within an organization or school structure.
- Background or interests of individuals (what types of things peak their interests).
- Facts about the organization. This is especially helpful if you are applying for a job.

Audience

To whom will you show your portfolio?

_____

_____

_____

_____

_____

Determine the Purpose, Objectives, Goals, and Outcomes for Your Portfolio

Based on who you have determined is your audience, it's time to decide on the purpose, objectives, goals, and outcomes of your portfolio. Choose one type of portfolio from the four categories and take a moment to jot down preliminary thoughts about the purpose, goals, and your desired outcome.

- MASTER PORTFOLIO
- ASSESSMENT PORTFOLIO
  __Academic
  __Technical
- CAREER PORTFOLIO
  __Resume-based
  __Project
  __Performance
- PERSONAL
  __Self-discovery
  __Scrapbook

Purpose

Why are you creating the portfolio for this audience?

_____

_____

_____

_____

_____

Goals and Objectives

What skills, competencies, and/or behaviors do you want to document?

_____

_____

_____

_____

_____

Desired Outcomes

What do you want to happen as a result of creating and showing your portfolio?

_____

_____

_____

_____

_____

Regardless of the type of portfolio, the process for creating one is the same. Once the prework is done, there are just three simple steps to actually creating a portfolio: collect, reflect, and assemble.

COLLECT

The first step in creating your portfolio is to begin collecting samples of your work or artifacts that show your accomplishments. You can choose to collect either purposefully or randomly.

If you decide to generate a list of items that show specific skills or meet predetermined requirements, you are collecting purposefully. You are looking for examples of your work with a specific purpose or outcome in mind.

If you are not sure what to include, don't worry about what you collect; just collect randomly. Basically, save everything. The best time to add an artifact to your folder is when it is first completed, so when in doubt add it to the collection. For example, if you write a good paper, report, or sales letter, put the original or a duplicate in the file. If you take pictures of an event that you worked on, make duplicates and put a set in your folder.

If you are assembling an Academic or Technical Portfolio, check with the teacher, school, or the governing body to determine what types of documents must be included.

Whichever way you choose to collect artifacts, you will want to start with a folder, binder, or designated file area. This will become your Master Portfolio. If you are using a file, set up folders for each of your skill areas. The easier and more accessible the file is, the greater chance you have of success. For each artifact, use the STAR technique to record information about the piece while it is fresh in your mind.

If you are creating a Resume-based Portfolio, first determine the skills you are looking for. Then think back to one or more times when you used that skill. Hopefully, you will be able to find an artifact that demonstrates your ability to use the skill in your work environment. If you don't have a specific example, there may be other ways that you can demonstrate your knowledge. For example, you can include a product logo or brochure and write an accomplishment statement next to it. This technique will also work if you have written something that would be considered confidential or proprietary, and cannot include an actual sample of the work. In this case, your "artifact" might be your statement or STAR along with the company's brochure or logo. Or, perhaps there is a news story about the organization that you can use.

REFLECT

The reflection is the most time-consuming and fun part of the process. Now that you've collected your artifacts, it's time to go through everything and look for patterns. Why did you save that particular item? What does it say about you? Why are you proud of that accomplishment? Is this the best example you have?

Sort the artifacts into piles. Do they naturally fall into logical groups? If you are assembling an Academic or Technical Portfolio, you will want to create your headings from the information given to you by your teacher or the criteria for credentialing.

Next, prioritize your artifacts by selecting those that are the most important to you, fulfill the requirements of the project, and are examples of work that you want to do again. For each section of your portfolio, you may want to include only the best two to four examples. But don't throw out the samples you didn't use in this portfolio. You may want to return them to your Master Portfolio so you can easily find them and use them in a different portfolio in the future.

The last step is to analyze your accomplishment statements to determine whether they can be more succinct. On a separate piece of paper, write a few concise sentences about the artifact that can be included in your portfolio. These statements can also be used on your resume, on a job interview, or in a performance review. If you've created a product as part of a team, include the names and roles of those team members. Your acknowledgment of others says a lot about your teamwork and collaboration.

ASSEMBLE

Now that you've selected your best artifacts, it's time to assemble your portfolio.

You may have a choice of creating a paper or an e-portfolio (electronic). A paper portfolio is one that has been assembled into a binder and is made up of actual papers, photographs, and artwork. An electronic portfolio includes scanned or uploaded papers, photographs, video, or sound clips that have been uploaded onto a Web site, CD, or DVD.

Who you plan to share your portfolio with will be your guide for which format is best. If you are creating the portfolio in an academic setting, you may be required to use the school's electronic portfolio system. Or, if you're an artist and want to share your portfolio with potential clients across the country, you might want to create an online portfolio for an Internet presence and also have a paper portfolio for when you meet with a client in person.

Paper portfolios may be better if you're creating a Resume-based Portfolio or if you're keeping a Project Portfolio. There are benefits and drawbacks to each option, which I'll cover later on in this section.

Assembling the Paper Portfolio

If you have chosen the paper portfolio, now is the time to head to an office supply or art supply store, where you can find all the materials you will need to assemble your portfolio.

Most portfolios are assembled in a binder with plastic sleeves. Sections are created by using tabs or colored paper. Depending upon the type of portfolio, you can be as creative and colorful as appropriate to the situation and the audience.

The most effective portfolios I've seen included the following:

- Cover artwork with your name and date
- Table of contents
- Purpose statement
- A brief overview and a listing of what is included in each section
- Brief reflection for each artifact

The way your portfolio looks says a lot about who you are. Is your portfolio neat and clean? Is it well organized and are artifacts easy to find? If I'm a prospective employer, would I be impressed with your portfolio or be concerned? With portfolios, the entire package is just as important as the actual artifacts themselves.

The Benefits   The first time you create a portfolio, you may find it easier to create a paper version. This will allow you to focus on the contents rather than the technology. Remember, you always have the option of converting your paper documents to electronic documents later by scanning them into electronic files. You may want to create a collage of artifacts by scanning a few of your documents and making a composite of multiple items such as awards, certificates, or photos.

Another benefit of a paper portfolio is that it gives you complete control when you share it with its intended audience. You can choose what you show someone and in what order. For example, if you are on a job interview, you can easily show one example in response to a specific question. It is also easy and quick to maintain your portfolio should you want to change items for different interviews.

Employers are concerned about computer viruses, so they may refuse to look at a DVD or CD-ROM. (More and more often, I'm finding that employers are no longer opening any e-mail attachments.) They also may not have the time to look at a Web site, so a paper portfolio is usually the best choice for a Resume-based Portfolio. It can be easier to share a paper portfolio with a group of people at one time rather than relying on technology being available during an interview. And remember, when interviewing you want the focus to stay on you, not be diverted to a projection or computer screen.

In reviewing many portfolios, both paper and electronic, I often find a paper portfolio more exciting. Perhaps it's because I can hold it in my hands and it seems to have more depth and energy and is more personal.

Drawbacks   There really aren't very many drawbacks to a paper portfolio. A paper portfolio may not allow you to show off your technology skills. And, if for some reason you were to loose your portfolio, it may be difficult to duplicate.

The Electronic Portfolio

In a sense, most high school and college students already have an electronic portfolio—a page on MySpace or Facebook. Students keep information about what's important to them, so you could consider it the ultimate Personal Portfolio! But some of the information found on these social networking Web sites is definitely *not* what employers want to see. As a matter of fact, a significant number of employers look at these sites during an employment background check. Pictures of drinking, partying, or sexual poses may provide the employer with information that doesn't reflect well on you and may prevent your employment. Even if you have deleted information from your site, it's possible that someone with good search techniques can still find the content.

Computer skills are a necessity in today's job market. A skillfully executed electronic portfolio is a wonderful way to show off your technology skills. Artists, for example, benefit from creating an electronic portfolio so that their work can be seen by a large number of potential clients in different parts of the country at once. For a monthly fee, Web sites such as *www.creativehotlist.com* will host an artist's portfolio and allow the individual to be included in a database that helps a potential client find artists with particular skills.

When writing this book, I did a Google search on student portfolios and found a site hosted by the University of Washington. The results of an electronic portfolio contest yielded wonderful portfolios from a variety of students with different objectives. Unfortunately, Web sites are often taken down. To find current examples of different types of electronic portfolios search for "student portfolios," "e-portfolios," or "electronic portfolios."

If you do a quick Google search for Web page hosting, you'll find many organizations that will help you find a domain name and host your site for a small monthly fee. You can either build your electronic portfolio from scratch, placing it on your own Web site, or you can use a template from your school or an outside source.

Benefits   There are three major benefits of an electronic portfolio. The first is the ability to show off your technical skills. The second is that an electronic portfolio helps you store easy-to-lose important documents and certifications that you may need later. Search the Internet and you'll find organizations that allow you to store copies of your documents on their Web servers. Unfortunately, some of us may be affected by a natural disaster, fire, or theft in which we could lose everything. Storing your important documents on a secure server away from home means you'd be able to again have copies of the documents, which could help you get back on your feet.

Some employers will not take the time to look at an electronic portfolio left behind after a job interview. If your resume lists your Web site, however, a curious hiring manager may take a look.

Drawbacks   One major drawback to the electronic portfolio is that you may not have the necessary technology skills or resources. In order to create an electronic portfolio you will need a computer, scanner, and perhaps a digital camera. If you're creating your own Web site, it may be necessary to be familiar with a Web design software program such as Dreamweaver or PageMill. In a job search situation, you should consider that a portfolio that doesn't use the medium well might work against you.

Privacy issues may also be of concern. If you post your resume with personal information on your Web site, you have little or no control over who views that information. Some high school portfolio programs require parents to sign a release before their child can post a resume and portfolio on the Internet.

Another drawback to posting your portfolio is that hiring managers in the initial stage of the hiring process don't want to see any personal information that may compromise their ability to view your information without discrimination. For example, hiring managers would not want to see a photograph of you and your family. They would also not want to see any artifacts that might indicate your political or religious affiliation.

If you are not sure whether to create a paper or electronic portfolio, you may want to review what you know about your audience. Does your audience require an electronic portfolio? How many people will you be presenting your portfolio to and in what time frame? Do you need to change items in your portfolio quickly? Will you be presenting your portfolio yourself or do you just want to give others access to look at it at their convenience?

Whether you decide to create a paper or electronic portfolio, the steps will still remain the same. Now it is time to make your final selection of materials. You may need to try two or three different arrangements before you get it just right. The reflection notes should help you create a story that flows smoothly and logically. If you need to send your portfolio to a group without personally presenting the portfolio, make sure you have adequately explained the items included. If you are assembling a Resume-based Portfolio, be selective, choosing the three to five samples in each category that best represent the skills you would like to use again in the future.

Show your portfolio to a few friends or your family to get their reaction. You may find that you would like to change a few items or move an artifact from one section to another to improve the flow.

SECTION IV

Portfolio Worksheets and Presentation Strategies

The following pages provide you with a framework to create and present your own portfolio.

1. Choose the portfolio category and type that you would like to create.
2. Answer the questions and check the appropriate boxes.
3. Add additional information that applies to your unique situation.
4. Have fun!

MASTER PORTFOLIO

Your Master Portfolio allows you to collect and organize all artifacts for use in other portfolios at a later date.

Audience

The audience for my Master Portfolio is:

_____

_____

_____

Purpose

The purpose of the Master Portfolio is to collect artifacts. Check each portfolio below for artifacts that you'd like to collect for:

❑ Academic Portfolio
❑ Technical Portfolio
❑ Resume-based Portfolio
❑ Project Portfolio
❑ Performance Portfolio
❑ Personal Portfolio or Scrapbook

Benefits

The benefit of creating a Master Portfolio is simply to have a consistent method for collecting artifacts that you can easily retrieve at a later date. Check all those below that apply to you:

❑ Allows me to collect artifacts that I may want at a later date.
❑ Artifacts are easily organized.
❑ I am able to replace an artifact with a better example.
❑ Artifacts are kept clean and neat for a professional appearance.
❑ Opportunity for me to reflect on all my accomplishments.
❑ Able to pull specific artifacts for specific portfolios.

Collect

Keep a binder, box, or file in an easily accessible place. With a Master Portfolio, you will keep all papers, drawings, photographs, and work samples. When in doubt, add something to your portfolio—it can always be deleted later. Preserve the artifacts by placing them in a plastic sheet so they don't become creased or crumpled.

Reflect

Be sure to capture the key elements or story with each artifact when you add something to the portfolio. Reflection isn't as important with the Master Portfolio. Later when you decide to use an artifact in another portfolio you'll reflect in context of all you've collected to determine which artifacts are the best to pull out for the specific portfolio you're creating.

Assemble

One of the easiest ways to keep your Master Portfolio is by month. However, any way that works best for you is fine. Having a general idea of where artifacts are within the portfolio is a good idea. At the end of the month or year, you may want to consider creating a table of contents for quick reference.

Presentation Notes

While you may not be presenting your Master Portfolio to anyone, you may be sharing it with a teacher, family member, friend, or counselor who is helping you with other portfolios. Before sharing your portfolio with someone, take the time to make sure that it is neat and that you have an idea where your best artifacts are located.

ASSESSMENT PORTFOLIO—ACADEMIC

Academic Portfolios may cover one class, one semester or quarter, one year, or even a two- to four-year period.

Audience

The audience for my Academic Portfolio is:

_____

_____

_____

Purpose

The purpose of the portfolio may vary. Check with your teacher or school to better understand the objectives of the portfolio. Usually, the purpose will be to assess learning over a specified period. Check each purpose below that pertains to you:

- ❏ Document my academic achievements
- ❏ Assess my academic and personal growth over time
- ❏ Motivate and encourage me to set goals
- ❏ Provide tangible evidence of my learning as a student
- ❏ Inform my parents, graduate school, or prospective employer of my skills and knowledge
- ❏ Help me learn the skills of reflection and self-evaluation
- ❏ Document my learning in areas that do not lend themselves to traditional assessment such as tests
- ❏ Facilitate communication with my parents

Benefits

There are many benefits to creating an Assessment Portfolio. Check all those below that apply to you:

- ❏ Opportunity to reflect on my academic and personal growth
- ❏ Increase my awareness of the knowledge and skills I have gained
- ❏ Generates satisfaction and pride in my accomplishments
- ❏ Helps me build connections between courses, cocurricular activities, and career opportunities
- ❏ Encourages me to view my course work as a whole instead of a series of unrelated classes
- ❏ Allows me to be assessed in an alternative way
- ❏ Opportunity for me to begin organizing my work and experiences
- ❏ Allows me to take responsibility for being an active, thoughtful participant in the analysis and assessment of my own learning

Collect

Keep a binder, box, or file and add papers, drawings, photographs, and report cards. Remember, not everything you collect will go into your portfolio. In some cases, your teacher may suggest items to include or have specific items that must be included. Here are some examples of items you may want to collect:

Elementary and High School

- Drafts of papers and the final graded version
- Art projects or photographs of art projects
- Class photographs
- Personal photographs of family and friends
- Report cards
- Tests
- Reading lists
- Programs from plays or events
- Flyers or brochures from organizations visited on field trips

College

- Syllabi
- Acceptance letters
- Dean's list certificates
- Unofficial transcripts
- Class lists
- Drafts and final versions of papers
- Exams or quizzes
- Biographies of professors
- Photographs or brochures from community service projects
- Performance review from your supervisor from your internship
- Programs from special events you attended
- Graduation program

Reflect

The first thing to do is refresh your memory on the guidelines established by your teacher or school. Now, begin to sort the materials you have collected. Look for patterns. Why did you keep that particular item? How do you feel about it? Does that item fulfill the requirements set by your teacher? Write a brief description of each artifact. At the end of the school year you'll be glad you took the time.

Assemble

Check with your teacher or school to determine what type of folder or container best meets the guidelines. Some schools will ask you to complete a paper portfolio, while others have created an electronic template for you to use when uploading or scanning your artifacts.

Now is the time to select the three, five, or seven best examples in each of the areas you have decided to highlight. (However, some teachers may ask you to include all your work—both good and bad.)

Presentation Notes

If you are creating an Assessment Portfolio for school, your teacher may have you present your portfolio in class or at a parents' night event. Usually you will get only five to ten minutes for your presentation. You will want to check with your teacher to see if there are presentation guidelines.

Because time will be limited, you'll want to create a brief speech with an opening, body, and close. Remember the adage of the three parts to a presentation: (1) tell them what you are going to tell them, (2) tell them, and then (3) tell them what you just told them. You may also want to have a strong opening that grabs them. It might be your statement of purpose or a poem that you've included in the portfolio. Because this is an Assessment Portfolio, you should also include what you learned as a result of creating a portfolio.

Most people don't enjoy giving presentations. You can gain confidence by practicing presenting your portfolio to family or friends first.

ASSESSMENT PORTFOLIO—TECHNICAL

A Technical Portfolio documents your skills and competencies that meet standard requirements of a professional association or governing body.

Audience

The audience for my Technical Portfolio is:

_____

_____

_____

Purpose

The purpose of a Technical Portfolio is to show samples of your work that meet and exceed the standards established by a professional association or governing body. This portfolio may be reviewed by a group of individuals who will determine your eligibility for certification or licensure.

Benefits

There are many benefits to creating a technical portfolio. Check all that apply to you:

❑ Documents your academic foundation
❑ Shows samples of actual work performed
❑ Allows you to reflect on your personal and professional accomplishments and growth
❑ Establishes your credibility as a professional in my given field
❑ Provides you with information about my credentials to share with potential and current clients
❑ Other _____

Collect

Create one file for each skill area or competency that the professional organization has set as a standard. If an artifact fits in more than one area, photocopy or make note of it and place a copy in each area. You may want to make a note on each copy reminding you of where you filed the original.

Because each profession has unique standards, it is difficult to create a list that is specific; however, there are skills that apply to almost all professions:

- Basic skills—reading, writing, mathematics
- Interpersonal skills—listening, teamwork
- Communication skills—presentation, sales, writing
- Managing work—time management, meeting deadlines
- Problem-solving skills—research, creativity
- Leadership—motivation, vision

Reflect

You will most likely collect more artifacts than you will need. The reflection process for a Technical Portfolio comes as you evaluate each artifact to determine whether or not it should be included. Check with the governing body to see whether there are guidelines as to the number of artifacts that must be included. If not, you may want to limit the number to three to five in each section. Remember, you won't be there to discuss each piece, so keep your portfolio manageable.

Some questions you may want to ask yourself as you reflect and select your artifacts are:

- Does this artifact meet the established requirements?
- Would another artifact better illustrate my skills?
- Am I proud of this accomplishment?
- Is there a good story to tell about this artifact?

Assemble

You may want to create a paper portfolio first. Once you have it just the way you want it, you can convert it into an electronic portfolio. Generally you will not be presenting your Technical Portfolio in person. Because you won't be there to explain each artifact, it is critical that you take extra care with your organization and reflection notes.

Be sure to include your personal information at the very beginning of the portfolio so that there is no confusion as to whose work is in the portfolio. You may even want to create a statement of originality and/or a nondisclosure agreement and place it in the front of the portfolio.

You will want to start your portfolio with a table of contents and perhaps even include a mini–table of contents for each section. Be sure to include a brief summary for each artifact.

Presentation Notes

If you are asked to present your portfolio, review the requirements of the governing body and learn as much as you can about the individuals to whom you will be presenting. Determine the amount of time you have for your presentation, and structure it so that you make sure you present the most impressive artifacts. Don't forget to include an opening that grabs their attention.

If you are not presenting your portfolio in person and your portfolio must stand on its own, provide a friend or colleague with the requirements and ask her to go through the portfolio as it would be reviewed by the governing body.

CAREER PORTFOLIO—RESUME-BASED

The Resume-based Portfolio is created to bring your resume to life. Many employers use behavioral interviewing to select the best candidates. Behavioral interviewing is based on the belief that past performance predicts future performance. A Resume-based Portfolio provides the employer with examples of your past successful efforts.

Audience

The audience for my Resume-based Portfolio is:

_____

_____

_____

Purpose

The purpose of a Resume-based Portfolio is to show samples of work that show your proficiency in key skills, competencies, and behaviors that are required for a specific job or career. This portfolio may be reviewed by one individual or a group of individuals as part of an interviewing process.

Benefits

There are many benefits to creating a Resume-based Portfolio. Check all that apply to you:

❑ Shows samples of actual work performed

❑ Allows you to reflect on your professional accomplishments and career growth

❑ Establishes your credibility as a professional in my given field

❑ Documents your academic foundation and your interest in keeping your skills current through continuing education

❑ Provides insight into your professional association memberships and affiliations

❑ Other _____

Collect

Determine which of your skills are the ones you want to use in the future. Match these to the required skills and behaviors you find in job descriptions or job postings. Highlight the skills and behaviors that are shared by you and the employer. You may want to look for similar jobs at other organizations and create a composite list of skills, competencies, and behaviors. Use this list to create one file for each skill area or competency. If an artifact fits in more than one area, photocopy or make note of it and place a copy in each area. You may want to make a note on each copy reminding you of where you filed the original.

Because each job requires unique skills, it is difficult to create a list that is specific; however, here are skills that apply to almost all jobs.

- Communication skills—oral, written
- Flexibility—open to change and new ideas
- Conflict management—resolves conflicts, strives for win-win solutions
- Creativity and innovation—develops new insights
- Customer focus—anticipates and meets needs of clients
- Process and product improvement—continually improves the quality of products and services
- Initiative, decisiveness, and self-direction—self-motivated, results oriented, makes sound decisions
- Diversity—able to work with and relate to diverse populations
- Teamwork—works well with others
- Project management—understands and follows process

Reflect

Before you begin the reflection phase of this portfolio, it is a good idea to bring your resume up to date. Remember that your resume is based on the future, not the past, and it prioritizes and highlights the skills you want to use in the future. Your Resume-based Portfolio does the same.

Some questions you may want to ask yourself as you select your artifacts are:

- Does this artifact show that I have the skills for this job?
- Would another artifact better illustrate my skills?
- Am I proud of this accomplishment?
- Is there a good story to tell about this artifact?
- Does this artifact support an accomplishment statement listed on my resume?

Assemble

As you plan this portfolio, think about how you will use it in a job interview. It will most likely be used in response to a behavioral interview question, such as: "Tell me about a time when you...."

Be sure to include your resume and references in your portfolio. You may also want to create a statement of originality and/or nondisclosure agreement and place it in the front of the portfolio so that there is no confusion as to whose work is included and so that you protect yourself from someone stealing your ideas.

When you are in the interview, you will want to be able to locate your artifacts quickly in response to specific questions. One way to do this is to start with a table of contents and include a table of contents for each section. You can also number and create a brief accomplishment statement for each artifact for quick reference.

You may want to create a paper portfolio first. Once you have it just the way you want it, you can convert it into an electronic portfolio if that is appropriate for the position you're seeking.

Presentation Notes

Although a Resume-based Portfolio helps you stand out from the competition, it is important to remember that it does not take the place of what you say and how you present yourself in the interview. Your portfolio should be used to support your responses to questions asked during the interview. You may want to say, "If you'd like to see examples of my work, I have my portfolio with me," or "If you are interested, I can leave you a CD-ROM of my portfolio and you can review it when it's convenient for you."

There is a possibility that it will not be appropriate for you to share your portfolio during the interview. Don't be discouraged. The confidence that you feel as a result of creating your portfolio and preparing for the interview will allow you to be more prepared and make a favorable impression.

CAREER PORTFOLIO—PROJECT

The Project Portfolio provides documentation of all aspects of a project including planning, execution, and evaluation. The Project Portfolio is the one type of portfolio that may include the work of an entire team rather than just one individual.

Audience

The audience for my Project Portfolio is:

_____

_____

_____

Purpose

The purpose of a Project Portfolio is to provide documentation for a historical record or so that another group may replicate the project.

Benefits

The benefits of creating a Project Portfolio are many. Check all that apply to your project:

❑ Provides a written historical record of the project.
❑ Organizes information about resources for easy access when you want to re-create the project
❑ Keeps track of the marketing information, invoices, and correspondence
❑ Provides place to document feedback and project evaluation
❑ Other _____

Collect

You will want to collect documents from all stages of the project, including defining the project, the project planning, implementing the plan, and completion and evaluation.

Because the first phase of project management is to define the project, write a brief description of the project's goals and objectives. You might include a brief write-up on all the team members, including their names, contact information, and background. If you have conducted market research or a pilot program, include the results.

The planning phase will most likely generate the majority of the artifacts. You can include the project's budget, time line, resource information, and performance standards. These will later be compared with the actual budget, time line, and resources used. Any marketing materials or correspondence generated should also be collected, because it will be very useful for another team to review before it begins to re-create the project.

Once the project has been completed, a written evaluation from the team as well as any participants or customers is very important. Comments from participants or customers might concentrate on the result of the project, while the team's evaluation might include what could be done differently if the project is repeated.

Reflect

As you look through all the artifacts you've collected, you may decide that it isn't necessary to keep all of them. For example, if your project was to conduct a workshop and each participant completed an evaluation, you can save space by creating a one- or two-page recap of the comments.

Some questions you may want to ask yourself as you select your artifacts are:

• Is this artifact part of the project management process?
• Would another artifact better illustrate the project?
• Can this artifact be summarized and still give a full picture of the process?
• Does this artifact duplicate another artifact?
• Would this artifact be helpful to another team?

Assemble

As you think about assembling this portfolio, consider how it could be used in the future. Place yourself in the position of someone looking at it in one to five years without the benefit of having someone from the original project available to answer questions.

One way of organizing the project is to create sections for each phase: the project definition and parameters, the project plan, implementation of the plan, completion and evaluation.

Subsections may be helpful for separating out the marketing materials, budget, resources, and time line.

Presentation Notes

Most Project Portfolios will not be formally presented. You may, however, be asked to give a short presentation on the project to another group. The first step is to determine how much time you have to give your presentation and who the audience is. Depending upon the audience, you might consider creating your presentation in PowerPoint. Key documents can be scanned and added to the presentation. If your project was an event, include photographs in the presentation. In some cases it may be appropriate to create a condensed version of your portfolio to hand out to all the audience members. Don't forget to take your portfolio to the presentation—someone may want to review the entire project binder.

CAREER PORTFOLIO—PERFORMANCE

The Performance Portfolio is created to help you document your performance at work.

Audience

The audience for my Performance Portfolio is:

_____

_____

_____

Purpose

The purpose of a Performance Portfolio is to provide samples of your current work that show you have met the goals and objectives that you set forth at the beginning of the review period.

Benefits

There are many benefits to creating a Performance Portfolio. Check all that apply to you:

- ❑ Shows samples of actual work performed
- ❑ Allows you to reflect on your professional accomplishments and career growth
- ❑ Establishes your credibility as a professional in your field
- ❑ Allows your manager to see the work you have completed
- ❑ Provides you with documentation to support your request for an increase in pay based on your achievements for the organization
- ❑ Other _____

Collect

The basis of the Performance Portfolio is your performance agreement or objectives. This is most effective when you and your manager sit down and discuss your performance goals at the beginning of the review period. You should also discuss how meeting your performance objectives will be measured. In some cases, specific work samples can be used as that documentation. In other cases, you may need to be sensitive to proprietary documents such as computer programs that you have written for your organization. Although they may be used in your portfolio, it should be made clear that they will not leave the company and be used in a Resume-based Portfolio.

Because each job has unique performance goals, it is difficult to create a list that is specific; however, here are examples of what might be included:

- Time management—a copy of your calendar showing how you manage your time
- Teamwork—a copy of the team charter or output from team meetings
- Communication skills—samples of letters to customers, memos, and presentations
- Technical skills—samples of finished products, product brochures, photographs of completed projects

Reflect

In many performance reviews, the manager prepares a review and meets with the employee. In this case, you will want to call the meeting and do a self-evaluation. Your first step is to review your performance plan and determine which artifacts best document your performance.

Some questions you may want to ask yourself as you select your artifacts are:

- Does this artifact show that I met my performance goals?
- Would another artifact better illustrate my skills?
- Am I proud of this accomplishment?
- Is there a good story to tell about this artifact?
- Can I show measurable results?

Assemble

Use your performance plan to determine your topic areas, then create a table of contents. In some cases you may need to create an artifact from pieces of work. You may also ask a peer or subordinates to write a short evaluation of your work to be included in the portfolio.

Presentation Notes

The first time you initiate and conduct your review meeting, both you and your supervisor may feel a bit awkward. To put you both at ease, explain to your supervisor at the beginning of the review period what you would like to do and why. Acknowledge that you understand that she may still need to fill out the standard form used by all employees in the organization, but that you would still like to showcase your work before the evaluation is completed.

In your initial meeting, you and your supervisor will discuss the organization's and the department's goals and objectives. Together you will agree on your specific goals and discuss what completion of those goals will look like. You may talk about resources you will need in completing the goals, and you may determine whether there are any barriers she could help remove.

A week before your review, schedule a meeting in a private place where there will be no interruptions. It's also a good idea to allow plenty of time. Because you are initiating this process, it is your meeting, so you set the tone.

Open your meeting by briefly reminding your supervisor of the agenda and the purpose of the meeting. Use your performance plan as the guide for discussion, sharing the artifacts in your portfolio when appropriate. Getting feedback is always difficult. Share your thoughts and feelings and remain open-minded to her point of view. Close the meeting by summarizing three to five of your most important accomplishments during the review period and the areas of improvement that you'd like to concentrate on in the next few months.

PERSONAL PORTFOLIO

The Personal Portfolio is created for you. It can include elements from all the portfolios that have already been covered, or it can have its own special focus. There are no restrictions. Be creative and have fun.

Audience

The audience for my Personal Portfolio is:

_____

_____

_____

Purpose

The purpose of this portfolio is to create a document that allows you to reflect on your life and that provides you with a deep sense of satisfaction and accomplishment.

Benefits

Gathering artifacts for a Personal Portfolio allows you to:

- ❏ Create a scrapbook of important events and accomplishments to share with others.
- ❏ Document your success and accomplishments in your academic life, professional life, and personal life.
- ❏ Keep track of your thoughts and goals while going through a major life transition.
- ❏ Impress a potential landlord with a rental portfolio that provides him with the information he needs in order to consider your application for tenancy.
- ❏ Other _____

Collect

Because this portfolio will most likely be created at home, you may want to keep a file on your desk or in your home office. It is a good idea to have an idea of the purpose of your portfolio; otherwise you may end up collecting much more than you can store. Or, you may already have cards, letters, photographs, and ticket stubs that are crying out to be organized in a binder. The fun of a Personal Portfolio is that it can be anything you want it to be.

Reflect

As with the other portfolios, reflection is the key. Take the time to write a brief description of events. If there are photographs, write down the date and location the picture was taken as well as the names of the people in the order they appear. (Think back on how fun it was to look at old family photographs with the names of distant relatives you never met!)

Don't overlook the power of writing brief reflections. You might talk about what made a dinner special or even include some thoughts about how you overcame a difficult time.

Assemble

You can assemble your Personal Portfolio in a binder with plastic sleeves or go to an art supply store for scrapbooking supplies, such as stickers, rubber stamps, marker pens, and colored paper. You can also find special scissors and hole punches to add interest to your pages. Have fun with your portfolio and be as creative and colorful as you want.

CONCLUSION

A portfolio is a powerful tool. Whether you use a portfolio in an academic setting, in the workplace, or at home with your family, this tool provides a rich experience for the reflection and presentation of your accomplishments. In my conversations with those who have created a portfolio, every individual has been grateful for the experience and has made the commitment to continue the process. I hope you enjoy creating your own portfolio.

APPENDIX

SUPPLY LIST

- File folder, file tote box, or banker's box
- Hanging file folders, standard size
- File folders
- Binder or notebook (you will need an extra-wide binder if you are using extra-wide tabs)
- Clear sheet protectors
- Extra-wide three-ring tabs with labels
- Paper (high quality)
- Colored paper
- Scissors
- Digital camera
- Access to scanner
- Archival tape

Example of Statement of Originality and Confidentiality

The artifacts included in this portfolio represent the work of (your name) and/or the work of individuals I have worked with. In the cases where the work of others is included, it has been included with permission of the original artist.

I respectfully request that the information contained in these documents not be duplicated or distributed without the express permission of the author.

Copyright © (Date) (Name). All rights reserved.

Exercise

Following is a job ad for a manager of strategic planning. In the space provided below the ad, list all the skills and behaviors of a successful candidate that you can find.

> *Job Ad—Manager of Strategic Planning* We're looking for the right person to analyze market potential and economics. You will work as a member of a multidisciplinary project team to evaluate program performance, develop business plan projections, and support strategic decision making. Strong project management and analytical skills are required. The ideal candidate will be customer-oriented with excellent communication and organizational skills. We're seeking a self-starter and problem-solver who is highly motivated and able to do more than "crunch numbers." Experience with Excel, Word, and PowerPoint is required. Travel is required.

Key Skills, Competencies, and Behaviors

Those I have:

_____

Those I want to use again:

_____

Those I don't want to use again:

_____

Those I need to learn:

_____

Action Words

When writing your resume, the following action words can be helpful in creating your accomplishment statements.

Accomplished	Equipped	Paid
Achieved	Established	Performed
Adapted	Evaluated	Persuaded
Adjusted	Expanded	Planned
Administered	Expedited	Presented
Advanced	Filed	Prioritized
Analyzed	Furthered	Processed
Assessed	Gained	Produced
Assisted	Generated	Programmed
Attained	Guided	Promoted
Authorized	Handled	Provided
Budgeted	Helped	Publicized
Built	Implemented	Recommended
Chaired	Improved	Reduced
Collaborated	Increased	Repaired
Combined	Initiated	Reported
Communicated	Instructed	Researched
Completed	Interviewed	Reviewed
Composed	Introduced	Revised
Conducted	Learned	Scheduled
Convinced	Led	Screened
Coordinated	Located	Served
Created	Maintained	Simplified
Delegated	Managed	Sold
Designed	Maximized	Spoke
Developed	Mediated	Strengthened
Directed	Modified	Supervised
Displayed	Motivated	Supported
Edited	Negotiated	Tabulated
Employed	Operated	Taught
Encouraged	Ordered	Trained
Enhanced	Originated	Updated
Enlarged	Organized	Wrote

PORTFOLIO CATEGORIES & TYPES

1. MASTER PORTFOLIO

Audience	Purpose	Type
Individual	Collect all artifacts which can later be transferred into one or more of the other portfolios.	Master

2. ASSESSMENT PORTFOLIOS

Audience	Purpose	Type
Faculty, student, family	An assessment tool used by the faculty or institution. Students show personal and academic growth and competency over a designated time period (class, semester, year).	Academic
Governing body or professional association	An assessment tool for certification or licensure. The governing body determines criteria for portfolio.	Technical

3. CAREER PORTFOLIOS

Audience	Purpose	Type
Potential employer or client	Supports your resume. Focuses on the skills, knowledge, and behaviors needed in a specific job or career. The individual determines what is included in the portfolio.	Resume-based
Organization	This portfolio documents a project from beginning to end. It may be used to help another group re-create a similar project in the future, or it may just act as a historical document. Rather than representing the work of only one individual, this portfolio represents the work of an entire team.	Project
Current employer, employee	An employee can use this portfolio to support a performance plan and performance review. The artifacts are used to document how an employee meets or exceeds her performance objectives.	Performance

4. PERSONAL PORTFOLIO

Audience	Purpose	Type
Individual	A Personal Portfolio may or may not be shared with others. This portfolio may include personal mementos as well as artifacts from any other type of portfolio.	Personal

ADDITIONAL READING

Alverno College. (1999). Diagnostic digital portfolio. Online: http://ddp.alverno.edu.

Bostaph, Charles and Vendeland, Roland. (2000). *The employment portfolio*. Upper Saddle River, NJ: Prentice Hall.

Bridges, William. (1994). *JobShift: How to prosper in a workplace without jobs*. Reading, MA: Addison-Wesley.

Department of Education, College of Notre Dame. (1990). *Developing as a professional education: A CND experience*. Belmont, CA.

Figler, Howard. (1979). *The complete job-search handbook* (3rd ed.). New York: Henry Holt.

Kimeldorf, Martin. (1994). *Creating portfolios: for success in school, work, and life*. Minneapolis: Free Spirit Publishing.

Kimeldorf, Martin (Ed.). (1996–1997). Portfolios [Special issue]. *Career Planning and Adult Development Journal* (V12, N4).

Nelles, Rick. (2001). *Proof of performance: how to build a career portfolio to land a great new job*. Manassas Park, VA: Impact Publications.

Straub, Carrie. (1996). *Creating a skills portfolio*. Menlo Park, CA: Crisp Publications.

Williams, Anna and Hall, Karen. (2001). *Creating your career portfolio: At a glance guide for students* (2nd ed.). Upper Saddle River, NJ: Prentice Hall.